Languages with Dany

Beginners' French

Danielle Harris

Published 2023 by Languages with Dany

ISBN: 9798392573318

For Charlotte

Table of Contents

Les salutations et les présentations (Greetings and introductions)	1
À la gare (At the train station)	3
À l'hôtel (At the hotel)	6
Au restaurant (At the restaurant)	12
Faire des courses ou faire du shopping (Going shopping)	16
Au bar (At the Bar)	22
La routine quotidienne et une journée à la ferme (Daily routine and a day at the farm)	25
Une visite chez le médecin (A visit to the Doctor's)	31
Régler la note (Checking out)	35
Dans le taxi (In the taxi)	37
À l'aéroport (At the airport)	39
Échanger les données personnelles (Exchanging personal details)	43
Au camping (At the campsite)	47
Le déménagement (Moving house)	53
Le temps (The weather)	56
Les prépositions de lieu (Prepositions of place)	59
L'utilisation du pronom 'on' (The use of the pronoun 'on')	61
L'impératif	62
les journées et les mois	64
Index of Vocabulary Topics	67

Le thème un

Les salutations et les présentations (Greetings and introductions)

Conversation une

Sandrine	Bonjour !	Hello!
Pierre	Bonjour ! Je m'appelle Pierre. Vous vous appelez comment ?	Hello! My name is Pierre. What is your name?
Sandrine	Je m'appelle Sandrine.	My name is Sandrine.
Pierre	Enchanté.	It is nice to meet you.
Sandrine	Enchantée.	It is nice to meet you.
Pierre	Ah ! Désolé ! Je dois partir ! Au revoir.	Oh! Sorry! I have to leave! Goodbye!
Sandrine	Au revoir ! À une prochaine fois.	Goodbye! I'll see you next time.

Conversation deux

Sandrine	Bonjour Pierre, vous allez bien ?	Hello Pierre! How are you?
Pierre	Oui, très bien merci. Et vous ?	I am very well, thank you. And yourself?
Sandrine	Oui, ça va. Vous êtes d'où ?	I am fine. Where are you from?
Pierre	Je suis anglais. Et vous êtes d'où ?	I am English. And where are you from?
Sandrine	Je suis française.	I am French.
Pierre	Ah ! Désolé ! Je suis en retard au travail !	Oh! Sorry! I am late for work!
Sandrine	Au revoir.	Goodbye.
Pierre	Au revoir. Bonne journée.	Goodbye. Have a good day.

Les nationalités

French is a language in which grammatical gender is a significant feature. This means that nouns (objects and concepts) have a gender, and adjectives (words which describe nouns) change depending on the gender of the noun they are describing. For example, if say a phrase in English such as **I am English**, in French this phrase will change depending on whether you are a man or a woman. Here is what that looks like in practice:

Les hommes (men)	Les femmes (women)	English
Je suis anglais	Je suis anglaise	I am English
Je suis français	Je suis française	I am French
Je suis gallois	Je suis galloise	I am Welsh
Je suis écossais	Je suis écossaise	I am Scottish

In the feminine forms, adding the 'e' means that you pronounce the 's' at the end of the word.

La liaison

Normally in French, you don't pronounce the last letter in the word. For example:

In 'Je suis', the second word is pronounced more like 'swee' than 'suees'

However! If the following word begins with a vowel, as in **je suis anglaise**, then you do pronounce the last letter, and so the whole phrase sounds like **je sweezonglez**.

La prononciation de lettres françaises

Many French letters are pronounced quite differently from English ones. One example is **R**. This should be pronounced from the back of the throat, not the front. In addition, the letter **U** is usually pronounced with the lips tightly pursed.

Conversation trois

Sandrine	Salut, Pierre. Ça va ?	Hi, Pierre. How's it going?
Pierre	Oui, ça va. Et toi ?	Yeah, it's going alright. How about you?
Sandrine	Oui, ça va bien. Tu es d'où ?	Yeah, I'm really good. Where are you from?
Pierre	Je suis anglais. Et tu es d'où ?	I'm English. And where are you from?
Sandrine	Je suis française.	I'm French.
Pierre	Tu habites où ?	Where do you live?
Sandrine	J'habite à Paris. Et toi ?	I live in Paris. How about you?
Pierre	J'habite à Manchester.	I live in Manchester.

La formalité

In French there are two main **registers**, that is, a **formal** and an **informal** variety. The first two conversations we looked at were in the **formal register**. This means that we used **vous** as the equivalent of **you**. Conversation three, however, is an introduction to the **informal register**, which means we used **tu** as the equivalent of **you**. You may have noticed that the verbs (words which describe actions) changed as well. We will learn more about this in future lessons.

Les expressions alternatives

In the conversations above, we looked at the informal version of **Where do you live?** and the formal version of **What is your name?** Here are their equivalents in the other register:

Vous habitez où ?	Where do you live? **(formal)**
Tu t'appelles comment ?	What is your name? **(informal)**

Le thème deux
À la gare (At the train station)

Conversation une

Pierre	Excusez-moi, Madame. Où est la gare ?	Excuse me, madam. Where is the train station?
L'employée de l'aéroport	Suivez les panneaux indicateurs là-bas à la gare.	Follow the signs over there to the train station.
Pierre	Ah ! Je n'avais pas vu les panneaux indicateurs ! Merci madame.	Oh! I hadn't seen the signs! Thank you, madam.
L'employée de l'aéroport	De rien monsieur. Au revoir.	You're welcome, sir. Goodbye.
Pierre	Au revoir.	Goodbye.

Conversation deux

Sandrine	Bonjour monsieur. Je voudrais un billet pour Paris s'il vous plaît.	Hello sir. I would like a ticket to Paris, please.
L'employé au guichet	Un aller-retour ou un aller-simple ?	A return or a single ticket?
Sandrine	Un aller-simple, s'il vous plaît.	A single, please.
L'employé au guichet	Oui, pour quand ?	OK, for when?
Sandrine	Le train prochain, si possible.	The next train if possible.
L'employé au guichet	Oui, c'est possible. Ça vous fait cinquante euros.	Yes, that's possible. That will be fifty euros.
Sandrine	Sur quel quai se trouve le train, s'il vous plaît ?	Which platform is the train on, please?
L'employé au guichet	Quai numéro trois.	Platform three.
Sandrine	Merci monsieur. Au revoir.	Thank you, sir. Goodbye.
L'employé au guichet	Au revoir.	Goodbye.

Quelle heure est-il ?

In French, the most common way to ask for the time is like this:

Quelle heure est-il ?

In French speaking countries they use the twenty-four-hour clock a lot more than we do in England, and it is written in a number of ways:

17:30

17.30

17h 30

The last one, although it looks strange to English speakers, is extremely common, and it gives us a clue about how we can pronounce it:

17h 30

Dix-sept heures trente

If someone asks you the time, though, you need to form a complete sentence, which looks like this:

Il est dix-sept heures trente.

Here, **Il est** means **it is**, so the full sentence translates to **it is half past five**.

Here is a list of numbers up to sixty to help you pronounce more times:

1 – un	*11 – onze*	*21 – vingt-et-un*	*31 – trente-et-un*	*41 – quarante-et-un*	*51 – cinquante-et-un*
2 – deux	*12 – douze*	*22 – vingt-deux*	*32 – trente-deux*	*42 – quarante-deux*	*52 – cinquante-deux*
3 – trois	*13 – treize*	*23 – vingt-trois*	*33 – trente-trois*	*43 – quarante-trois*	*53 – cinquante-trois*
4 – quatre	*14 – quatorze*	*24 – vingt-quatre*	*34 – trente-quatre*	*44 – quarante-quatre*	*54 – cinquante-quatre*
5 – cinq	*15 – quinze*	*25 – vingt-cinq*	*35 – trente-cinq*	*45 – quarante-cinq*	*55 – cinquante-cinq*
6 – six	*16 – seize*	*26 – vingt-six*	*36 – trente-six*	*46 – quarante-six*	*56 – cinquante-six*
7 – sept	*17 – dix-sept*	*27 – vingt-sept*	*37 – trente-sept*	*47 – quarante-sept*	*57 – cinquante-sept*
8 – huit	*18 – dix-huit*	*28 – vingt-huit*	*38 – trente-huit*	*48 – quarante-huit*	*58 – cinquante-huit*
9 – neuf	*19 – dix-neuf*	*29 – vingt-neuf*	*39 – trente-neuf*	*49 – quarante-neuf*	*59 – cinquante-neuf*
10 – dix	*20 – vingt*	*30 – trente*	*40 – quarante*	*50 – cinquante*	*60 – soixante*

Conversation trois

Sandrine	Bonjour monsieur. Je voudrais deux billets pour Paris s'il vous plaît.	Hello, sir. I would like two tickets to Paris, please.
L'employé au guichet	Aller-retour ou aller-simple ?	Return or single tickets?
Sandrine	Deux aller-retours, s'il vous plaît.	Two returns, please.
L'employé au guichet	Oui, pour quand ?	OK. When for?
Sandrine	Le train prochain, si possible.	The next train if possible.
L'employé au guichet	Oui, c'est possible.	Yes, that's possible.
Sandrine	À quelle heure part le train ?	What time does the train leave?
L'employé au guichet	À dix-sept heures trente. Vous arrivez à Paris à dix-huit heures.	At five thirty pm. You arrive in Paris at six o'clock.
Sandrine	Combien ça coute ?	How much does that cost?
L'employé au guichet	Ça coute cinquante euros. Vous payez comment ? En espèce ou par carte ?	It costs fifty euros. How are you paying? In cash or by card?
Sandrine	Je paye par carte. Sur quel quai se trouve le train, s'il vous plaît ?	I'll pay by card. What platform does the train depart from?
L'employé au guichet	Quai numéro trois.	From platform three.
Sandrine	Merci monsieur. Au revoir.	Thank you, sir. Goodbye.
L'employé au guichet	Au revoir.	Goodbye.

Le thème trois
À l'hôtel (At the hotel)

Conversation une

Réceptionniste	Bonjour Madame, Monsieur. Je peux vous aider ?	Hello madame, sir. Can I help you?
Sandrine	Bonjour. Je m'appelle Madame Laurent. Nous avons une réservation pour sept nuits.	Hello. My name is Mrs Laurent. We have a reservation for seven nights.
Réceptionniste	Ah ! Voilà la réservation. Sept nuits et une chambre avec une salle de bain.	Oh! Here's your reservation. Seven nights and a room with a bathroom.
Sandrine	Super, merci.	Great, thanks.
Réceptionniste	Vous avez la chambre dix-huit, au premier étage.	You have room eighteen, on the first floor.
Sandrine	Merci. Et à quelle heure est le petit déjeuner ?	Thank you. And what time is breakfast?
Réceptionniste	Le petit déjeuner est de huit heures à dix heures dans la salle à côté de la réception.	Breakfast is served from eight to ten in the room next to reception.
Sandrine	Merci Madame.	Thank you, madame.

À quelle heure… ?

In the first conversation, above, you saw this question:

À quelle heure est le petit déjeuner ?

This was used to ask what time breakfast was served. But, you can ask what time other things are happening using 'à quelle heure… ?'. For example, in the previous topic, we saw this question:

À quelle heure part le train ?

What time does the train leave?

Les genres de noms

In French, all **nouns** (words for objects, concepts, and people) have genders. They are either masculine or feminine. In English, we have one definite article, **the**, and one indefinite article, **a**. In French, there is one indefinite article and one definite article for each gender of noun:

Masculine indefinite article ('a') – un

Masculine definite article ('the') – le

Feminine indefinite article ('a') – une

Feminine indefinite article ('the') – la

Here are some examples of how they are used:

une/la chambre (feminine) – a/the bedroom

une/la réservation (feminine) – a/the reservation

un/le petit déjeuner (masculine) – a/the breakfast

un/le train (masculine) – a/the train

If a noun begins with a **vowel** or an **h**, the definite article (**the**) is written as **l'**, with an apostrophe. Here are some examples:

un hôtel / l'hôtel (a hotel / the hotel) - masculine

un étage / l'étage (a floor / the floor) – masculine

une étagère / l'étagère (a shelf / the shelf) – feminine

Les nombres ordinaux

first	premier (m) / première (f)	1st	1er (m) / 1ère (f)
second	deuxième	2nd	2ème
third	troisième	3rd	3ème
fourth	quatrième	4th	4ème
fifth	cinquième	5th	5ème
sixth	sixième	6th	6ème
seventh	septième	7th	7ème
eighth	huitième	8th	8ème
ninth	neuvième	9th	9ème
tenth	dixième	10th	10ème

Quel(le)

We've seen how you can ask about the time using 'À quelle heure... ?', but you can also use a similar format to ask what floor something is on:

À quel étage est ma chambre ?

(What floor is my room on?)

The response to this from a hotel receptionist would be:

Votre chambre est au (premier/deuxième etc.) étage.

(Your room is on the (first/second etc.) floor.)

Conversation deux

Réceptionniste	Voilà la chambre. Il y a un grand lit, une fenêtre, une petite table, et une salle de bain avec une douche et une toilette.	Here is your room. There is a large bed, a window, a small table, and a bathroom with a shower and a toilet.
Pierre	Oh non ! Excusez-moi, mais il n'y a pas de serviettes !	Oh no! Excuse me, but there are no towels!
Réceptionniste	Je suis désolée.	I'm sorry.
Pierre	Et, il n'y a pas de shampooing. Je voudrais du shampooing.	And there is no shampoo. I would like some shampoo.
Réceptionniste	Tout de suite, Monsieur.	Straight away, sir.
Pierre	Et la clé ?	And the key?
Réceptionniste	Voilà la clé, numéro dix-huit.	Here is your key, number eighteen.

Furniture Vocabulary

armchair	un fauteuil (m)
bed	un lit (m)
table	une table (f)
bedside table	une table de chevet (f)
coffee table	une table basse (f)
dining-room table	une table de salle à manger (f)
bookcase	une bibliothèque (f)
carpet	un tapis (m) / une moquette (f)
chair	une chaise (f)
couch / sofa	un canapé (m)
sofa-bed	un canapé-lit (m)
cupboard	un placard (m)
curtain	un rideau (m)
curtains	des rideaux (plural)
desk	un bureau (m)
drawer	un tiroir (m)
chest of drawers	une commode (f)
fireplace	une cheminée (f)
mirror	un miroir (m)
shelf	une étagère (f)
wardrobe	une armoire (f)

Il y a…

When we want to say **there is…** or **there are…** in French, we use **Il y a**. For example:

Dans la chambre, il y a une petite table.

(In the bedroom, there is a small table.)

If you want to say **there isn't** or **there aren't**, you can use **il n'y a pas**. You also have to change the **un/une** to **de**. For example:

Il n'y a pas de douche dans la salle de bain.

There isn't a shower in the bathroom.

Conversation trois

Réceptionniste	Excusez-moi, vous voulez laisser la clé ?	Excuse me, do you want to leave your key?
Sandrine	Oui, merci.	Yes, thank you.
Réceptionniste	Merci à vous. Et vous allez où aujourd'hui ?	No, thank you! And where are you going today?
Sandrine	Nous allons à la Tour Eiffel et nous allons au Louvre.	We're going to the Eiffel Tower and we're going to the Louvre.
Réceptionniste	C'est formidable. Amusez-vous bien ! Bonne journée.	That's fantastic! Have fun! Have a good day.
Sandrine	Bonne journée.	Have a good day.

Pronouns

The verb **aller** means **to go**, but the word changes depending on who you're referring to. For example:

Je	vais	I	go / am going
Tu	vas	you (informal)	go / are going
Il/elle	va	he/she	goes / is going
Nous	allons	we	go / are going
Vous	allez	you (formal)	go / are going
Ils/elles	vont	they (m) / they (f)	go / are going

Here is an example of the verb used in a sentence:

Je vais à la Tour Eiffel

(I am going to the Eiffel Tower.)

Tu vas à la Tour Eiffel.

(You are going to the Eiffel Tower. – informal version.)

The verb **avoir** means **to have**. This verb also changes depending on who you're referring to, but it does so in a different way:

j'	ai	I	have
tu	as	you (informal)	have
il/elle	a	he/she	has
nous	avons	we	have
vous	avez	you (formal)	have
ils/elles	ont	they (m) / they (f)	have

Here are some examples of this verb being used in a sentence:

J'ai un grand chapeau.

(I have a large hat)

Elles ont un grand chapeau.

(They have a large hat.)

Another important verb is **être**, which means **to be**:

je	suis	I	am
tu	es	you (informal)	are
il/elle /on	est	he/she	is
nous	sommes	we	are
vous	êtes	you (formal)	are
ils/elles	sont	they (m) / they (f)	are

Here are some examples of this verb being used in a sentence:

Je suis heureux (m) / heureuse (f).

(I am happy.)

Nous sommes heureux (mixed group or group of men) / heureueses (group of women).

(We are happy.)

All of the above verbs are **irregular**, which means they all change in a unique way that isn't the same as most verbs. Here is what a regular verb, **manger** (**to eat**) looks like:

je	mange	I	eat / am eating
tu	manges	you (informal)	eat / are eating
il/elle /on	mange	he/she	eats / is eating
nous	mangeons	we	eat / are eating
vous	mangez	you (formal)	eat / are eating
ils/elles	mangent	they (m) / they (f)	eat / are eating

Here are some examples of this verb being used in a sentence:

Elle mange le gâteau.

(She is eating the cake.)

Vous mangez le gâteau.

(You are eating the cake. – formal version.)

Le thème quatre
Au restaurant (At the restaurant)

Conversation Une

Serveur	Bonsoir Monsieur, Madame.	Good evening, sir, madam.
Pierre	Bonsoir Monsieur. Je voudrais une table pour deux personnes, pour dîner, s'il vous plaît.	Good evening, sir. I would like a table for two for dinner, please.
Serveur	Vous avez une réservation ?	Do you have a reservation?
Pierre	Non, je n'ai pas de réservation.	No, I don't have a reservation.
Serveur	Pas de problème. Voici une table pour deux personnes, et voilà la carte.	No problem. Here is a table for two, and here is the menu.
Pierre	Merci Monsieur.	Thank you, sir.

La négation

During this dialogue, you heard Pierre tell the waiter that he didn't have a reservation:

Je n'ai pas de réservation.

(I don't have a reservation.)

If you wanted to tell the waiter that you **did** have a reservation you could say this:

J'ai une réservation.

(I have a reservation.)

To make this positive sentence negative, we put a **n** and an apostrophe in front of the verb (**ai** – **have**) and a **pas** after it. We used **n** and an apostrophe because the verb starts with a vowel, **a**, but when the verb starts with a consonant, we use **ne**:

Je suis serveuse.

(I am a waitress.)

Je ne suis pas serveuse.

(I am not a waitress.)

Note that when you use an indefinite article (**un** or **une**) in a positive sentence, this becomes **de** in a negative sentence:

J'ai une clé.

(I have a key.)

Je n'ai pas de clé.

(I don't have a key.)

Conversation Deux

Serveur	Monsieur, Madame, vous avez choisi ?	Sir, Madam, have you chosen?	
Sandrine	Je voudrais le menu à quinze Euros s'il vous plaît.	I would like the fifteen Euro menu, please.	
Serveur	Oui. En Entrée ?	OK. For starters?	
Sandrine	Je voudrais le pâté.	I would like the pate.	
Serveur	Et en plat principal ?	And for main course?	
Sandrine	Je voudrais le steak frites.	I would like the steak and chips, please.	
Serveur	Bien Madame, quelle cuisson ?	OK, Madam. How would you like it cooked?	
Sandrine	Bien cuit, s'il vous plaît. Non, à point, s'il vous plaît.	Well-done, please. No, medium, please.	
Serveur	En dessert ?	For dessert?	
Sandrine	Une glace à la vanille.	Vanilla ice cream.	

Food Vocabulary

(La nourriture / Les aliments)

Les Fruits (m) – Fruit		Les produits (m) laitiers - Dairy products	
l'abricot (m)	apricot	le beurre	butter
l'ananas (m)	pineapple	la crème	cream
la banane	banana	le fromage	cheese
la cerise	cherry	la glace	ice cream
le citron	lemon	le lait	milk
la fraise	strawberry	le yaourt	yogurt
la framboise	raspberry		
le melon	melon		
l'orange (m)	orange		
le pamplemousse	grapefruit		
la pastèque	watermelon		
la pêche	peach		
la poire	pear		
la pomme	apple		
le raisin	grape		

Les légumes (m) – Vegetables

l'ail (m)	garlic
les asperges (f)	asparagus
la carotte	carrot
le céleri	celery
le champignon	mushroom
le chou-fleur	cauliflower
le concombre	cucumber
la courgette	courgette
les épinards (m)	spinach
le haricot	bean
la laitue	lettuce
l'oignon (m)	onion
les petits pois (m)	peas
le poivron	bell pepper
la pomme de terre	potato
la tomate	tomato

La viande - Meat

l'agneau (m)	lamb
le steak	steak
la dinde	turkey
les escargots (m)	snails
le jambon	ham
le lapin	rabbit
le poisson	fish
le porc	pork
le poulet	chicken
le bœuf	beef
le saucisson	sausage
le veau	veal

Le dessert – Dessert

le biscuit	biscuit
les bonbons (m)	sweets
le chocolat	chocolate
le gâteau	cake
la tarte	tart

Les Autres - Others

la confiture	jam
les frites (f)	chips
l'huile d'olive (f)	olive oil
le miel	honey
la moutarde	mustard
un œuf, des œufs	egg, eggs
le pain	bread
les pâtes (f)	pasta
le poivre	pepper
le riz	rice
le sel	salt
le sucre	sugar
la tartine	toast

Conversation Trois

Serveur	Bonsoir Monsieur, Madame.	Good evening, Sir, Madam.
Pierre	Bonsoir Monsieur. Je voudrais une table pour trois personnes, pour déjeuner, s'il vous plaît.	Good evening, Sir. I would like a table for three for lunch, please.
Serveur	Vous avez une réservation ?	Do you have a reservation?
Pierre	Non, je n'ai pas de réservation.	No, I don't have a reservation.
Serveur	Pas de problème. Voici une table pour trois personnes.	No problem. Here is a table for three.
Pierre	Vous avez la carte ?	Do you have a menu?
Serveur	Oui, bien sûr. Voilà.	Yes, of course. Here you are.
	Un peu plus tard…	
Serveur	Monsieur, Madame, vous avez choisi ?	Sir, Madam, have you chosen?
Sandrine	Je voudrais le menu à vingt Euros.	I would like the twenty Euro menu, please.
Serveur	Oui. En Entrée ?	OK. For starters?
Sandrine	Je voudrais le pâté.	I would like the pate.
Serveur	Et en plat principal ?	And for main course?
Sandrine	Je voudrais le steak frites.	I would like the steak and chips, please.
Serveur	Bien Madame, quelle cuisson ?	OK, Madam. How would you like it cooked?
Sandrine	Saignant, s'il vous plaît. Non, à point, s'il vous plaît.	Rare, please. No, medium, please.
Serveur	En dessert ?	For dessert?
Sandrine	Une glace au chocolat.	Chocolate ice cream.
	Un peu plus tard encore…	
Serveur	Vous avez fini ?	Have you finished?
Sandrine	Oui, c'était délicieux. L'addition, s'il vous plaît.	Yes, it was delicious. Could we have the bill please?

Le thème cinq (La première partie)
Faire des courses ou faire du shopping (Going shopping)

Conversation une (à l'épicerie)

Sandrine	Bonjour Monsieur	Hello, Sir.
Vendeur	Bonjour Monsieur, Madame. Comment puis-je vous aider ?	Hello, Sir, Madam. How can I help you?
Sandrine	Oui. Je voudrais des oranges, s'il vous plaît.	Yes. I would like some oranges, please.
Vendeur	Un kilo ? Deux kilos ?	A kilo? Two kilos?
Sandrine	Un kilo, et je voudrais aussi une boîte de sardines, un litre de lait, un kilo de farine, et un paquet de spaghettis.	I would also like a tin of sardines, a litre of milk, a kilo of flour, and a packet of spaghetti.
Vendeur	Quelle marque vous préférez ?	What brand do you prefer?
Sandrine	Thirion, si vous l'avez.	Thirion, if you have it.
Vendeur	Voilà. Vous voudriez autre chose ?	Here you go. Would you like anything else?
Sandrine	Oui. Combien coûtent les fraises ?	Yes. How much do the strawberries cost?
Vendeur	Quatre euros la barquette de deux cent cinquante grammes. Elles sont chères, mais elles sont délicieuses !	Four Euros for a two hundred and fifty gram punnet. They are expensive, but they are delicious!
Sandrine	Bon, une barquette, s'il vous plaît.	OK, one punnet, please.
Vendeur	Ça sera tout ?	Is that everything?
Sandrine	Oui, c'est combien ?	Oui. How much is it?
Vendeur	Ça fait douze euros. Voilà votre ticket.	That will be twelve euros. Here is your receipt.

L'emballage et les quantités

un kilo / le kilo	a kilo / the kilo
une boîte / la boîte	a tin / the tin
un litre / le litre	a litre / the litre
un paquet / le paquet	a packet / the packet
une marque / la marque	a brand / the brand
une barquette / la barquette	a punnet / the punnet
un gramme / le gramme	a gram / the gram

Les adjectifs

Adjectives are words which describe nouns (things, objects, concepts etc). For example, in the phrase **the expensive strawberries**, the adjective is **expensive** because it describes the strawberries (the noun).

In French, adjectives must agree with the noun in number and in gender. This means that if the noun is plural, the adjective must be plural, and if the noun is feminine, then the adjective must also be feminine. We saw this in the first conversation, above:

Les fraises sont chères, mais elles sont délicieuses !

In this example, **fraises** is a feminine, plural noun, and so **chères** and **délicieuses** are feminine, plural adjectives.

In general, if we want to use an adjective in its feminine form, we can just add an **e** onto its masculine form. Sometimes we need to add an accent as well:

Le citron cher (le citron is <u>masculine</u> and <u>singular</u>)

La fraise chère (la fraise is <u>feminine</u> and <u>singular</u>)

If we want to use an adjective in its plural form, we usually add an **s** onto its singular form. This is combined with adding an **e** (and possibly an accent) for plural feminine nouns:

Les citrons chers (les citrons is <u>masculine</u> and <u>plural</u>)

Les fraises chères (les fraises is <u>feminine</u> and <u>plural</u>)

Usually, French adjectives are placed **after** the noun that they describe. In addition, if we want to describe a noun which we have already introduced and say something like **they are expensive** or **it is expensive**, then we need to use a **pronoun** (she, he, they etc) that agrees with the noun in number and gender:

Le citron cher -> Il est cher (masculine/singular)

La fraise chère -> Elle est chère (feminine/singular)

Les citrons chers -> Ils sont chers (masculine/plural)

Les fraises chères -> Elles sont chères (feminine/plural)

Here are some more adjectives that we can use with food:

délicieux (m/s), délicieuse (f/s), délicieux (m/pl), délicieuses (f/pl)	delicious
acide (m+f/s), acides (m+f/pl)	sour
aigre (m+f/s), aigres (m+f/pl)	sour
sucré (m/s), sucrée (f/s), sucrés (m/pl), sucrées (f/pl)	sweet
salé (m/s), salée (f/s), salés (m/pl), salées (f/pl)	salty/savoury
piquant (m/s), piquante (f/s), piquants (m/pl), piquantes (f/pl)	spicy
chaud (m/s), chaude (f/s), chauds (m/pl), chaudes (f/pl)	hot (temperature, **not** spicy)
froid (m/s), froide (f/s), froids (m/pl), froides (f/pl)	cold
amer (m/s), amère (f/s), amers (m/p), amères (f/pl)	bitter
frais (m/s), fraîche (f/s), frais (m/pl), fraîches (f/pl)	fresh
gras (m/s), grasse (f/s), gras (m/pl), grasses (f/pl)	fatty
sain (m/s), saine (f/s), sains (m/pl), saines (f/pl)	healthy
cher (m/s), chère (f/s), chers (m/pl), chères (f/pl)	expensive

Conversation deux (à la boulangerie)

Vendeuse	Bonjour monsieur. Vous désirez ?	Hello Sir. What would you like?
Pierre	Bonjour madame. Je voudrais trois croissants au beurre, un pain aux raisins et un pain au chocolat, s'il vous plaît.	Hello Madam. I would like three butter croissants, a pain aux raisin, and a pain au chocolat, please.
Vendeuse	Oui, ça sera tout ?	OK, is that everything ?
Pierre	Qu'est-ce que vous avez comme tartes ?	What kinds of tarts do you have?
Vendeuse	J'ai des tartes aux pommes ou des tartes aux fraises.	I have apple arts and strawberry tarts.
Pierre	Je prends une tarte aux fraises.	I'll have a strawberry tart.
Vendeuse	Oui. C'est pour combien de personnes ?	OK. How many people is it for?
Pierre	Pour deux personnes.	For two people.
Vendeuse	Voilà monsieur. Quinze euros cinquante.	Here you go Sir. Fifteen euros fifty.
Pierre	Voilà.	Here you are.
Vendeuse	Merci monsieur, au revoir.	Thank you, Sir. Goodbye.
Pierre	Au revoir, bonne journée.	Goodbye. Have a good day.

Conversation trois (au magasin de vêtement)

Vendeur	Bonjour, je peux vous aider ?	Hello. Can I help you?
Sandrine	Oui, je cherche une veste…	Yes, I'm looking for a jacket.
Vendeur	Ce serait pour une occasion particulière ?	Is it for a particular occasion?
Sandrine	Non, c'est pour mettre tous les jours.	No, it's for everyday wear.
Vendeur	Quelle est votre taille ?	What size are you ?
Sandrine	Moyenne.	Medium.
Vendeur	Oui, alors, j'ai celle-ci… Le tissu est léger. Vous pouvez la porter pour toutes les occasions.	OK. I have this one here… The fabric is light. You can wear it for any occasion.
Sandrine	Oui, je cherche quelque chose de plus décontracté.	OK. I'm looking for something a little more casual.
Vendeur	Alors, j'ai ce modèle en coton.	OK, I have this one in cotton.
Sandrine	Oui, je l'aime bien.	Yes, I like that a lot.
Vendeur	Vous voulez l'essayer ?	Would you like to try it on?
Sandrine	S'il vous plaît.	Please.
Vendeur	Attendez… voilà.	Wait a moment… Here you go.
Sandrine	Oui, elle me plaît bien. Elle est à combien ?	Yes, I like that a lot. How much is it?
Vendeur	Cent euros.	One hundred euros.
Sandrine	Vous l'avez dans d'autres couleurs?	Do you have it in any other colours?
Vendeur	En moyenne, il me reste noir, gris ou marron.	In medium, I have got black, grey, or brown left.
Sandrine	Je vais essayer la noire.	I'll try the black.
Vendeur	Tenez.	Here you are.
Sandrine	Merci.	Thank you.
Vendeur	Ça vous va très bien.	That looks good on you.
Sandrine	Oui, je crois que je vais la prendre.	Yes, I think I'll take it.
Vendeur	Vous ne regretterez pas votre achat, c'est un bon produit. Vous désiriez autre chose ?	You won't regret your purchase! It's a good product. Would you like anything else?
Sandrine	Non, merci.	No, thank you.
Vendeur	Alors, suivez-moi, on va passer à la caisse. Vous payez par carte ?	OK, follow me and we'll go to the till. Are you paying by card?
Sandrine	Oui… tenez.	Yes… Here you go.
Vendeur	Merci, vous pouvez taper votre code. Merci. Voilà Madame.	Thank you. You can enter your PIN. Thank you. Here you go, madame
Sandrine	Merci.	Thank you.
Vendeur	De rien. Au revoir et Bonne journée.	You're welcome. Goodbye, and have a good day.
Sandrine	Au revoir.	Goodbye.

Clothes Vocabulary
(Les vêtements)

cardigan	un gilet / un cardigan
coat	un manteau
jacket	une veste
jeans	un jean
pyjamas	un pyjama
trousers	un pantalon
raincoat	un imperméable
shorts	un short
jumper/sweater	un pull
t-shirt	un tee-shirt
boots	des bottes (f)
sandals	des sandales (f)
shoes	des chaussures (f)
trainers	des baskets (f)/ des chaussures de sport (f)
socks	des chaussettes (f)
blouse	un chemisier
dress	une robe
skirt	une jupe
suit	un costume
shirt	une chemise
tie	une cravate

Using Colours as Adjectives

When we employ colours as adjectives (words used to describe objects, or 'nouns'), they behave in the same way as most other French adjectives. They are placed after the noun (the object), and they take on both a masculine or feminine form, and a singular or plural form, which match the gender of the noun. For example:

Un manteau vert – masculine/singular

(A green coat)

Une jupe verte – feminine/singular

(A green skirt)

Des manteaux verts (masculine/plural)

(Some green coats)

Des jupes vertes (feminine/plural)

(Some green skirts)

Note that when we use a plural noun, we must make **both** the noun and the adjective plural by adding the appropriate letters to each word. Most of the time, this will mean an 's' is added to both words, however some plural nouns have different letters added to them, or none at all. For example, the plural of 'manteau', is 'manteaux'.

Here is a list of how French colours change when they are used to describe masculine and feminine nouns:

Masuline Singular Adjective	Feminine Singular Adjective	Masculine Plural Adjective	Feminine Plural Adjective	English Adjective
bleu	bleue	bleus	bleues	blue
rouge	rouge	rouges	rouges	red
vert	verte	verts	vertes	green
jaune	jaune	jaunes	jaunes	yellow
blanc	blanche	blancs	blanches	white
noir	noire	noirs	noires	black
gris	grise	gris	grises	grey
rose	rose	roses	roses	pink
violet	violette	violets	violettes	purple
marron	marron	marron	marron	brown
orange	orange	orange	orange	orange

Le thème six

Au bar (At the bar)

Conversation une

Pierre	Bonsoir Monsieur ! Je voudrais une table pour quatre personnes.	Good evening, Sir! I would like a table for four people.
Serveur 1	Bonsoir Monsieur ! Bien sûr, vous pouvez prendre la table numéro cinq, juste à votre gauche.	Good evening, Sir! Of course, you can have table five, just to your left.
Pierre	Merci !	Thank you!
Serveur 1	Veuillez-vous asseoir et le serveur va vous joindre dans un instant.	Please take a seat and a waiter will be with you in a moment.
Pierre	D'accord, merci.	OK, thank you.
Henri	Alors, qu'est-ce que vous prenez Pierre ?	So, what are you having, Pierre?
Pierre	Pour moi, une limonade parce que je conduis. Et toi, Sandrine ?	For me, a lemonade because I'm driving. And for you, Sandrine?
Sandrine	Moi, une bière naturellement.	For me, a beer of course.
Henri	Moi, je ne sais pas… un vin rouge, ou un vin blanc… Non, un cognac, c'est mieux. Et pour toi Claire ?	For me, I don't know… A red wine or a white wine… No, a brandy, that's better. And for you, Claire?
Claire	Pour moi, je prends un café au lait.	For me, I'll have a white coffee.
Serveur 2	Bonsoir, messieurs-dames. Qu'est-ce que vous désirez ?	Good evening, ladies and gentlemen. What would you like?
Sandrine	Alors, une bière.	Right, a beer.
Serveur 2	Bouteille ou pression ?	In a bottle or on draught?
Sandrine	Pression s'il vous plaît.	On draught, please.
Pierre	Une limonade pour moi, et pour toi Claire ?	A lemonade for me, and for you, Claire?
Claire	Un café au lait pour moi, et un cognac pour mon mari.	A white coffee for me and a brandy for my husband.
Serveur 2	D'accord. C'est tout ?	OK. Is that everything?
Pierre	Oui, c'est tout. Merci.	Yes, that's everything. Thank you.
Serveur 2	J'arrive tout de suite messieurs-dames.	I'll be back straight away, ladies and gentlemen.

Les Boissons

une limonade	lemonade
un jus de pomme/pamplemousse/tomate/ananas	apple/grapefruit/tomato/pineapple juice
un jus d'orange	orange juice
une eau	water
une eau du robinet	tap water
une eau minérale	mineral water
une eau gazeuse	sparkling water
une eau plate	still water
un chocolat chaud	hot chocolate
un café	coffee
un café au lait	white coffee
un thé	tea
un thé vert	green tea
un vin blanc/rouge/rosé	white/red/rosé wine
un champagne	champagne
une bière	beer
un cidre	cider
un Coca	Coke
un Coca light	diet Coke
un cognac	brandy
une vodka	vodka
un whisky (single malt)	whisky (or single malt whisky)
un gin (tonic)	gin (and tonic)
un rhum (blanc/brun)	(white/dark) rum
une bouteille de…	a bottle of…
un verre de…	a glass of…

Les questions ouvertes et fermées

In French, as in English, you can ask **closed questions**, which have a **yes** or **no** answer, or you can ask **open questions**, which require a longer, more detailed answer. To ask closed questions in French, we use **est-ce que**. For example:

Est-ce que tu bois de la bière ?

(Do you drink beer?)

This question has a **yes** or **no** answer, but to make our French a little richer, we can add some more words to make our reply sound less curt:

Q: Est-ce que tu bois de la bière ?

A: Oui, je bois de la bière. OR Non, je ne bois pas de la bière.

To ask open questions, we use **qu'est-ce que**. For example:

Qu-est-ce que tu bois ?

(What are you drinking?)

Here, the question requires a more detailed answer because you have to specify what you are drinking:

Q: *Qu-est-ce que tu bois ?*

A: *Je bois de la bière. (I'm drinking beer)*

Note: When talking about what you're drinking, you use *de la* with feminine nouns such as *la bière*, and you use *du* with masculine nouns such as *le vin*.

Le verbe 'boire'

je bois	I drink *or* I am drinking
tu bois	you drink *or* you are drinking (informal)
elle / il boit	she / he drinks *or* she / he is drinking
nous buvons	we drink *or* we are drinking
vous buvez	you drink *or* you are drinking (formal)
elles / ils boivent	they drink *or* they are drinking

Le thème sept

La routine quotidienne et une journée à la ferme (Daily routine and a day at the farm)

Conversation une

This conversation isn't really a conversation at all; Sandrine and Pierre are getting ready for their day out at a farm on the outskirts of Paris, and so Sandrine is telling Pierre about how her daily routine works. This is what she says:

Sandrine : *Normalement, je me lève à sept heures trente.*

(Normally, I get up at seven-thirty.)

Puis, je me brosse les dents, je me douche, je me lave le visage, je m'habille, et je me maquille.

(Then, I brush my teeth, I shower, I wash my face, I get dressed, and I put on my makeup.)

À huit heures quinze, je prends le petit déjeuner, et je vais au travaille vers huit heures trente.

(At eight-fifteen, I have breakfast, and I go to work at around eight-thirty.)

Le soir, je rentre chez moi vers dix-sept heures trente. Une fois à la maison, je prends le dîner, je me repose, et je me couche vers vingt-trois heures.

(In the evening, I go home at about five-thirty. Once home, I have dinner, I relax, and I go to bed at around eleven o'clock.)

Then Pierre tells Sandrine about his daily routine:

Pierre : *Normalement, je me lève à sept heures quinze.*

(Normally, I get up at seven-fifteen.)

Puis, je me brosse les dents, je me douche, je me rase, et je m'habille.

(Then, I brush my teeth, I shower, I shave, and I get dressed.)

À huit heures, je prends le petit déjeuner, et je vais au travaille vers huit heures quinze.

(At eight o'clock, I have breakfast, and I go to work at around eight-fifteen.)

Le soir, je rentre chez moi vers dix-sept heures. Une fois à la maison, je prends le dîner, je me repose, et je me couche vers vingt-deux heures trente.

(In the evening, I go home at about five o'clock. Once home, I have dinner, I relax, and I go to bed at around ten-thirty.)

Les verbes pronominaux

In previous lessons, we've looked at some regular verbs (words that describe actions), and how they change according to who the speaker is talking about:

travailler (to work)

je	travaille	I	work
tu	travailles	you (informal)	work
elle/il	travaille	she/he	works
nous	travaillons	we	work
vous	travaillez	you (formal or plural)	work
elles/ils	travaillent	they (feminine/masculine)	work

Travailler is a regular verb, which means the word forms (the **conjugations**) change according to a pattern which is the same as in other regular verbs. For example, here's another regular verb.

penser (to think)

je	pense	I	think
tu	penses	you (informal)	think
elle/il	pense	she/he	thinks
nous	pensons	we	think
vous	pensez	you (formal or plural)	think
elles/ils	pensent	they (feminine/masculine)	think

Notice how the letters in bold change in the same way for each verb, depending on whether the person being spoken about (the **subject**) is **je**, **tu**, **nous**, etc.

Some verbs are **irregular**, which means they don't follow any kind of pattern at all. For example:

aller (to go)

je	vais	I	go
tu	vas	you (informal)	go
elle/il	va	she/he	goes
nous	allons	we	go
vous	allez	you (formal or plural)	go
elles/ils	vont	they (feminine/masculine)	go

Most of the verbs which we saw in **conversation une**, are **pronominal verbs**, or more specifically, **reflexive verbs**, which means they describe actions that a person does on themselves. These verbs have an extra part added onto them called a **reflexive pronoun**. For example:

se lever (to get up)

French Pronoun	French Reflexive Pronoun	French Verb Conjugation	English Pronoun	English Verb Conjugation
je	me	Lève	I	get up
tu	te	lèves	you (informal)	get up
elle/il	se	lève	she/he	gets up
nous	nous	levons	we	get up
vous	vous	levez	you (formal or plural)	get up
elles/ils	se	lèvent	they (feminine/masculine)	get up

Note that the main part of the verb changes in the same way are a regular verb, but watch out for the forms that require an accent!

The reflexive pronouns roughly translate to **myself, yourself, herself** etc. This means that when you use a reflexive verb, you're saying that you do something to yourself. For example:

Je me lève.

(I get myself up.)

You have seen a reflexive verb before; when you say what your name is, or ask someone for their name:

Je m'appelle Sandrine.

(I am called Sandrine. Or more literally: I call myself Sandrine)

Vous vous appelez comment ?

Tu t'appelles comment ?

(What is your name? Or more literally: How do you call yourself?)

Here is the complete verb table for the verb **s'appeler**:

s'appeler (to be called, or more literally, to call yourself)

French Pronoun	French Reflexive Pronoun	French Verb Conjugation	English Pronoun	English Verb Conjugation
je	m'	appelle	I	am called
tu	t'	appelles	you (informal)	are called
elle/il	s'	appelle	she/he	is called
nous	nous	appelons	we	are called
vous	vous	appelez	you (formal or plural)	are called
elles/ils	s'	appellent	they (feminine/masculine)	are called

Note how the reflexive pronouns **me**, **te**, and **se** are shortened to **m'**, **t'**, and **s'** because **appeler** and its conjugations begin with a vowel, **a**.

À la ferme

To say what animals are on a farm, we can use **il y a**:

À la ferme, il y a…

(On the farm, there is…)

Les Animaux

un taureau	a bull
une vache	a cow
un ver de terre	an earthworm
une abeille	a bee
un agriculteur/une agricultrice	a farmer
un chat/une chatte	a cat
un âne	a donkey
un canard	a duck
un chien/une chienne	a dog
un poisson	a fish
un renard	a fox
une grenouille	a frog
une oie	a goose
une chèvre	a goat
un cheval	a horse
une poule	a hen
une souris	a mouse
une autruche	an ostrich
une chouette effraie	a barn owl

un cochon	a pig	
un poney	a pony	
un coq	a cockerel	
une mouche	a fly	
un mouton	a sheep	
une chauve-souris	a bat	
une guêpe	a wasp	
un escargot	a snail	
un écureuil	a squirrel	
un dindon	a turkey	

Le comparative et le superlative

We can compare attributes in people, animals, and objects by using **the comparative** and **the superlative**. The comparative is used to compare things. To employ it, we use the following constructions:

plus + adjective + que

moins + adjective + que

For example:

L'écureuil est plus ancien que le dindon.

(The squirrel is older than the turkey.)

L'écureuil est moins lourd que le dindon.

(The squirrel is less heavy than the turkey.)

If you want to describe something that has the **most** or **least** of an attribute, you can use the **superlative**. This uses the following construction:

La chauve-souris est la plus intelligente.

(The bat is the most intelligent.)

Le mouton est le moins intelligent.

(The sheep is the least intelligent.)

Here are some adjectives that you can use to compare the farm animals listed above:

French Masculine Adjective	French Feminine Adjective	English Adjective
âgé	âgée	old
jeune	jeune	young
lourd	lourde	heavy
léger	légère	light
tendre	tendre	gentle
intelligent	intelligente	intelligent
notoire	notoire	notorious

Le thème huit

Une visite chez le médecin (A visit to the Doctor's)

Conversation une

Secrétaire		Cabinet médical de Belleville, bonjour.	Belleville Surgery, hello.
Pierre		Bonjour. Je vous appelle pour prendre rendez-vous avec un médecin.	Hello, I am calling to book an appointment with a doctor.
Secrétaire		D'accord. Ne quittez pas.	Ok. Please hold.
		Quelques instants plus tard…	*A few moments later…*
Secrétaire		Merci d'avoir patienté. Le docteur Boisaubert est disponible demain à 14h et jeudi à 9h30. Quel créneau horaire vous conviendrait ?	Thank you for waiting. Doctor Boisaubert is available tomorrow at 2 p.m. and Thursday at 9:30 a.m. Which time slot works for you?
Pierre		Demain à 14h me convient.	Tomorrow at 2 p.m. works for me.
Secrétaire		Votre nom, monsieur ?	Your surname, sir?
Pierre		Martin. Et le prénom c'est Pierre.	Martin. And the first name is Pierre.
Secrétaire		D'accord Monsieur Martin. Je confirme votre rendez-vous avec le docteur Boisaubert pour demain à 14h.	Ok Mr. Martin. I have booked your appointment with Doctor Boisaubert for tomorrow at 2 p.m.
Pierre		Merci beaucoup.	Thank you very much.
Secrétaire		Je vous en prie. Bonne journée, au revoir.	You are welcome. Have a nice day, goodbye.
Pierre		De même, au revoir.	You too, goodbye.

When speaking on the phone, the following phrases can be useful:

Can you repeat that, please? – Pouvez-vous répéter, s'il vous plaît ?

I don't understand – Je ne comprends pas.

Conversation deux

Dr Boisaubert	Bonjour monsieur. Alors, qu'est-ce-qui vous amène ?	Hello, Sir. So, what brings you here?
Pierre	Bonjour Docteur. Eh bien, ça fait plusieurs jours que j'ai mal partout.	Hello, doctor. Well, I've had pain all over for the last few days.
Dr Boisaubert	Où avez-vous mal exactement ?	Where is the pain exactly?
Pierre	Dans la nuque, les bras, les épaules, les mains, les jambes, les pieds ... partout !	At the back of my neck, my arms, my shoulders, my hands, my legs, my feet... everywhere!
Dr Boisaubert	Aha... Avez-vous pris votre température ?	Aaah... Have you taken your temperature?
Pierre	Oui, j'ai de la fièvre.	Yes, I have a fever.
Dr Boisaubert	Alors, veuillez-vous asseoir là. Ouvrez la bouche et dites « aaaaaah ».	OK, please sit here. Open your mouth and say 'aaaaaah'.
Pierre	« Aaaaaah »	'Aaaaah'
Dr Boisaubert	Hummm... je ne vois rien d'anormal, il ne semble pas y avoir d'inflammation. Avez-vous également mal au ventre ?	Hmmm... I don't see anything abnormal, it doesn't seem to be inflamed. Do you also have stomach pain?
Pierre	Euh... non, docteur.	Erm... no, doctor.
Dr Boisaubert	Des migraines ? Des nausées ? Des soucis de digestion ?	Migraines? Nausea? Digestion problems?
Pierre	Non, aucune.	No, none.
Dr Boisaubert	Ressentez-vous une fatigue anormale ?	Do you feel unusually tired?
Pierre	Oui, je suis très fatigué	Yes, I'm very tired.
Dr Boisaubert	Eh bien, vous avez de la fièvre virale, mais ne vous inquiétez pas. Je vais vous donner une ordonnance, vous serez très bien.	OK, you have a viral fever, but don't worry. I am going to give you a prescription, you will be fine.
Pierre	Merci docteur, au revoir.	Thank you. Goodbye.
Dr Boisaubert	Au revoir.	Goodbye.

Le Vocabulaire Médical

I have asthma	Je suis asthmatique
I have a cold	Je suis enrhumé(e)
I am constipated	Je suis constipé(e)
I have diabetes	Je suis diabétique
I am pregnant	Je suis enceinte
I have been sunburned	Je suis brulé(e) par le soleil
I am (very) tired	Je suis (très) fatigue(e)

The vocabulary above is all used with the verb **être** (**to be**). Here is a reminder of how we use this verb:

je	suis	I am
tu	es	you are (informal)
il/elle	est	he/she is
nous	sommes	we are
vous	êtes	you are (formal)
ils/ells	sont	they are

I have arthritis	J'ai de l'arthrite
I have diarrhea	J'ai la diarrhée
I am dizzy	J'ai le vertige
I have a fever	J'ai de la fièvre
I have the flu	J'ai la grippe
I am having a heart attack	J'ai une crise cardiaque
I have heartburn	J'ai des brûlures d'estomac
I have hemorrhoids	J'ai des hémorroïdes
I have an infection	J'ai une infection
I have sinusitis	J'ai de la sinusite

The vocabulary above is all used with the verb **avoir** (**to have**). Here is a reminder of how we use this verb:

j'	ai	I have
tu	as	you have (informal)
il/elle	a	he/she has
nous	avons	we have
vous	avez	you have (formal)
ils/elles	ont	they have

To talk about pain, you use **avoir mal à**:

I have an earache	J'ai mal à l'oreille
I have a headache	J'ai mal à la tête
I have a stomachache	J'ai mal à l'estomac
I have a toothache	J'ai mal aux dents

To tell a doctor that you need something you use **avoir besoin de**:

I need an inhaler	j'ai besoin d'un inhalateur
I need a prescription	j'ai besoin d'une ordonnance
I need stitches	j'ai besoin de points de suture
I need an ultrasound	j'ai besoin d'une échographie
I need an x-ray	j'ai besoin d'une radio

Parts of the Body

head	la tête
finger	le doigt
stomach	le ventre / l'estomac (m)
knee	le genou
leg	la jambe
foot	le pied
hand	la main
arm	le bras
shoulder	l'épaule (f)
hair	les cheveux (m)
eye	l'œil (m)
eyes	les yeux (m)
ears	les oreilles (f)
mouth	la bouche
teeth	les dents (f)
nose	le nez

Conversation trois

Docteur		Bonjour [**Monsieur/Madame**]. Alors, qu'est-ce-qui vous amène ?	Hello [**Sir, Madame**]. So, what brings you here?
Patient(e)		Bonjour Docteur. [**Say what the problem is.**]	Hello, Doctor. [**Say what the problem is.**]
Docteur		Hummm… Y a-t-il autre chose qui vous inquiète ?	Hmmm… Is there anything else worrying you?
Patient(e)		Euh… [**Tell the doctor that you have another problem.**]	Erm…. [**Tell the doctor that you have another problem.**]
Docteur		Eh bien, ne vous inquiétez pas. Je vais vous donner une ordonnance, vous serez très bien.	OK, don't worry. I am going to give you a prescription, you will be fine.
Patient(e)		Merci docteur, au revoir.	Thank you Doctor. Goodbye.
Docteur		Au revoir.	Goodbye.

Le thème neuf
Régler la note (Checking out)

Conversation une

Réceptionniste	Bonjour Monsieur Martin. Comment puis-je vous aider ?	Hello, Mr. Martin. How can I help you?
Pierre	Bonjour. Nous sommes prêts à régler la note.	Hello. We're ready to check out.
Réceptionniste	Bien sûr… alors… c'était une chambre double pendant sept nuits avec petit déjeuner. C'est ça ?	Of course… so… it was a double room from seven nights with breakfast. Is that right?
Pierre	Oui, c'est exact.	Yes, that's correct.
Réceptionniste	Tout s'est bien passé ?	Was everything OK for you?
Pierre	Oui, l'hôtel est super. Le seul inconvénient est que nous avions demandé une chambre avec deux lits et nous avons eu un lit double, mais ce n'est pas grave.	Yes, the hotel is great. The only problem is that we'd asked for a room with two beds, and we had one double bed, but it's not important.
Réceptionniste	Je suis désolée. Nous étions complets toute la semaine ! Est-ce que je peux faire autre chose pour vous aider ?	I'm sorry. We were full all week! Is there anything else I can help you with?
Pierre	Oui, pourriez-vous m'appeler un taxi ?	Yes, could you call me a taxi?
Réceptionniste	Tout de suite, Monsieur. Au revoir.	Straight away, sir. Goodbye.
Pierre	Au revoir.	Goodbye.

Le Conditionnel, vouloir et pouvoir

In English, we use **would** to ask for things more politely. For example:

I would like two tickets for the three-thirty screening of Spiderman 18.

This is more polite than:

I want two tickets for the three-thirty showing of Spiderman 18.

There is a similar way of making requests more polite in French, but in French there is no equivalent of the word **would**. Instead, we use a different form of the verb called **the conditional**. For example, below is a table of the regular present tense and conditional forms of the verb **vouloir** (**to want**):

French Pronoun	French Present Tense	English Present Simple	French Conditional	English Conditional
je	veux	I want	voudrais	I would like
tu	veux	you want (informal)	voudrais	you would like (informal)
il/elle /on	veut	he/she wants	voudrait	he/she would like
nous	voulons	we want	voudrions	we would like
vous	voulez	you want (formal)	voudriez	you would like (formal)
ils/elles	veulent	they want	voudraient	they would like

In a similar way, it is more polite to use **could** rather than **can** when asking people to do things. For example:

Could you call me a taxi?

This is more polite than:

Can you call me a taxi?

The verb **can** is unusual in English in that it does not pair with the word **would** to make its conditional form. Below is a table of the regular present tense and conditional forms of the French verb **pouvoir** ('to be able to' or 'can'):

French Pronoun	French Present Tense	English Present Simple	French Conditional	English Conditional
je	peux	I can	pourrais	I could
tu	peux	you can (informal)	pourrais	you could (informal)
il/elle /on	peut	he/she can	pourrait	he/she could
nous	pouvons	we can	pourrions	we could
vous	pouvez	you can (formal)	pourriez	you could (formal)
ils/elles	peuvent	they can	pourraient	they could

Here are some examples of how the conditional form of **pouvoir** can be used to make polite requests:

Pourriez-vous nous aider ?

(Could you help us?)

Pourrais-tu me passer le sel ?

(Could you pass me the salt?)

Le thème dix
Dans le taxi (In the taxi)

Conversation une

Sandrine	Bonjour monsieur.	Hello, Sir.
Le chauffeur de taxi	Bonjour monsieur, madame. Où allez-vous aujourd'hui ?	Hello, Sir, Madame. Where are you going today?
Sandrine	À l'aéroport s'il vous plaît.	To the airport, please.
Le chauffeur de taxi	Charles de Gaulle, Orly, ou Beauvais ?	Charles de Gaulle, Orly, or Beauvais
Sandrine	Charles de Gaulle, s'il vous plaît.	Charles de Gaulle, please.
Le chauffeur de taxi	D'accord… Allons-y !	OK… Let's go!
Sandrine	C'est combien pour aller à l'aéroport ?	How much is it to the airport?
Le chauffeur de taxi	Euh… Je ne sais pas.	Erm… I don't know.
Sandrine	Ah… Mettez le compteur s'il vous plaît.	Ah… Please turn on the meter.
Le chauffeur de taxi	Bien sûr.	Of course.
Sandrine	Est-ce que vous connaissez la route ?	Do you know the way?
Le chauffeur de taxi	Euh, non…	Erm, no.
Sandrine	Est-ce que nous sommes perdu ?	Are we lost?
Le chauffeur de taxi	Très probablement, oui…	Very possibly, yes.
Sandrine	D'accord, je vais utiliser Google Maps…	OK, I'm going to use Google Maps…

Le futur proche

When you are **certain** that something is going to happen in the future, that you **intend** to do something, and/or that an action is going to be fairly immediate, you can use the **near future tense** or **le future proche**. To do this, we use a construction which is similar to the English use of 'going to'. For example:

I am going to use Google Maps.

In French we use the verb **aller** (to go) to do this. The table below is a reminder of how **aller** is used:

je	vais	I	go / am going
tu	vas	you (informal)	go / are going
il/elle /on	va	he/she	goes / is going
nous	allons	we	go / are going
vous	allez	you (formal)	go / are going
ils/elles	vont	they (m) / they (f)	go / are going

To use **aller** to talk about the future, we use the appropriate form of **aller** with another verb in its infinitive, or main form:

Je   vais   utiliser   Google Maps.

I   am going   to use   Google Maps.

Here are some other examples of sentences using **aller** to describe the future:

Tu vas appeler un taxi.

(You are going to call a taxi.)

Nous allons manger ce gâteau.

(We are going to eat this cake.)

Elle va regarder la télévision.

(She is going to watch television.)

Les directions

Où se trouve…?	Where is…?	La prochaine rue à gauche/droite.	The next road on the left/right
Où est…?	Where is…?	Allez au coin de la rue.	Go around the corner.
Au bout de la rue…	At the end of the road…	Au rond point…	At the roundabout…
Au carrefour…	At the crossroads…	…prenez la première/deuxième/ troisième sortie.	…take the first/second/ third exit.
…prenez la première/deuxième/ troisième rue…	…take the first/second/third road…	Vous êtes arrivé(e) à destination.	You have arrived at your destination.
…à gauche.	…left.		
…à droite.	…right.		
Continuez tout droit et…	Carry straight on and…		
…tournez à droite /gauche.	…turn right/left.		

Le thème Onze
À l'aéroport (At the airport)

Conversation une

Pierre	Bonjour.		Hello.
Assistant	Bonjour, puis-je avoir vos billets d'avion et vos passeports s'il vous plaît ?		Hello, can I have your tickets and your passports please?
Pierre	Les voici.		Here you go.
Assistant	Merci. Vous avez des bagages ?		Thank you. Do you have any luggage?
Pierre	Oui, nous avons deux bagages à main et deux valises.		Yes, we have two items of hand luggage and two suitcases.
Assistant	D'accord. Veuillez poser vos valises sur la balance s'il vous plaît. Vous n'avez aucun objet interdit dans vos valises ?		OK. Please place your cases on the scales. Do you have any forbidden objects in your cases?
Pierre	Euh, non, aucun.		Erm, no, none.
Assistant	D'accord, c'est bon. Voici vos cartes d'embarquement. Vous embarquerez à douze heures cinq, porte numéro neuf. Je vous souhaite un bon voyage.		OK, that's all fine. Here are your boarding passes. Your plane boards at five past twelve, gate nine. I hope you have a good trip.
Pierre	Merci, au revoir.		Thank you, goodbye.

Conversation deux

Sandrine	Bonjour Madame. Notre vol a été annulé ce matin alors je voudrais changer nos billets s'il vous plaît.	Hello, Madame. My flight has been cancelled this morning, so I would like to change my tickets, please.
Assistant	Bonjour Madame, Monsieur. Est-ce que je peux voir vos passeports et vos billets s'il vous plaît ?	Hello, Madam, Sir. Can I see your passports and your tickets, please?
Sandrine	Oui, bien sûr. Voilà !	Yes, of course. Here you are.
Assistant	D'accord. Je peux voir que vous avez réservé un aller-retour ?	OK. I can see that you have reserved a return ticket?
Sandrine	Oui, nous retournons en Angleterre. J'aimerais juste changer l'heure de départ, si possible toujours en classe économique. À quelle heure part le prochain vol ?	Yes, we're going back to England. I would just like to change the departure time, and if possible stay in economy class. What time does the next flight leave?
Assistant	Le prochain vol est en trente minutes, à quatorze heures quinze. Voulez-vous le réserver ?	The next flight is in thirty minutes, at quarter-past two. Would you like to book it?
Sandrine	Oui, s'il vous plaît.	Yes please.
Assistant	Est-ce que vous avez des bagages en soute ?	Do you have any checked-in luggage?
Sandrine	Oui. Je les ai déjà donnés à un autre assistant.	Yes, I have already given it to another assistant.
Assistant	D'accord. Je les transférerai à votre nouveau vol. Et voici vos cartes d'embarquement.	OK. I'll transfer it to your new flight. And here are your boarding passes.
Sandrine	Où est la porte d'embarquement, Madame ?	Where is the departure gate, Madam?
Assistant	Le numéro de votre porte d'embarquement est écrit sur vos cartes. C'est juste en face de la cafétéria.	The number of your departure gate is written on your passes. It's just opposite the cafeteria.
Sandrine	Ah, d'accord. Merci.	Ah, OK. Thank you.
Assistant	Bon voyage !	Have a good flight!
Sandrine	Merci. Au revoir.	Thank you. Goodbye.
Assistant	Au revoir.	Goodbye.

La possession

In le thème onze, conversation deux, you saw some examples of people talking about things which belonged to them, or to others:

Notre vol a été annulé

(*Our* flight has been cancelled)

Est-ce que je peux voir vos passeports ?

(Can I see *your* passports?)

In French, possession can work quite differently than in English, because if you possess multiple objects, then both the object, and the word which shows possession (the possessive adjective) must be plural. For example:

Mon passeport

(*My* passport)

Mes passeports

(*My* passports)

In addition, it is the gender of the object, and not the gender of the person who possesses it which is important:

Son passeport (passport is masculine)

(*His* passport OR *her* passport)

Sa carte d'embarquement (carte d'embarquement is feminine)

(*Her* boarding pass OR *his* boarding pass)

Here is a complete table of all the possessive adjectives in French:

With masculine singular noun	With feminine singular noun	With plural noun (masculine or feminine)	English meaning
mon	ma	mes	my
ton	ta	tes	your (informal)
son	sa	ses	his/her
notre	notre	nos	our
votre	votre	vos	your (formal)
leur	leur	leurs	their

If a feminine noun begins with a **vowel** or an **h**, then you use the masculine possessives. For example:

Mon assiette (feminine noun)

My plate

Stationary Vocabulary for Possessives Game

a pencil case	une trousse
a pen	un stylo
scissors	des ciseaux (m)
a rubber	une gomme
a ruler	une règle
a paperclip	un trombone
a hole punch	un perforateur
keys	des clés (f)

To say that an item/some items belong to someone, you can use pronouns and the verb **être** along with the possessive adjective:

Elle est sa carte d'embarquement

(It is her/his boarding pass)

Elles sont mes valises

(They are my suitcases)

As a reminder, here is the full table of all the forms of **être**:

je	suis	I	am
tu	es	you (informal)	are
il/elle	est	he/she	is
nous	sommes	we	are
vous	êtes	you (formal)	are
ils/elles	sont	they (m) / they (f)	are

Le thème douze
Échanger les données personnelles (Exchanging personal details)

Conversation une

Pierre	Alors, parle-moi un peu de ta famille.	So, tell me a little bit about your family.
Sandrine	Je vis à la maison avec mon père et ma mère. J'ai un grand frère et une grande soeur. Je suis la dernière de la famille.	I live with my father and my mother. I have a big brother and a big sister. I am the youngest of the family.
Pierre	Quelle grande famille ! Moi je suis tout seul. Nous sommes trois à la maison avec mon père et ma mère. Par contre j'ai beaucoup de cousins et de cousines.	What a big family! I am an only child. There are three in our house, with my father and my mother. However, I have a lot of cousins.
Sandrine	Ah oui tu as combien de cousins et cousines ?	Really? How many?
Pierre	J'ai cinq cousins et quatre cousines. Je les vois souvent quand je vais chez mes grands parents le dimanche. Et toi as-tu des cousins ?	I have nine cousins. Five boys and four girls. I often see them when I go to my grandparents on Sundays. Do you have any cousins?
Sandrine	Oui j'ai trois cousins et j'ai aussi deux neveux et une nièce parce que mon grand frère est marié et il a deux garçons. Ma grande soeur est mariée aussi et elle a une fille.	Yes I have three cousins. I also have two nephews and a niece because my big brother is married and he's got two boys. My big sister is also married and she's got a girl.
Pierre	Vous êtes nombreux, vous devez faire beaucoup d'activités tous ensemble alors.	There is a lot of you! You must do a lot of activities together, then.
Sandrine	Oui nous organisons des sorties tous ensemble. Je vais t'inviter un jour.	Yes, we organise family outings all together. I will invite you someday.

La famille

father	le père
mother	la mère
son	le fils
daughter	la fille
brother	le frère
sister	la sœur
husband	le mari
wife	la femme
grandparents	les grands-parents
grandfather	le grand-père
grandmother	la grand-mère
great grandfather	l'arrière-grand-père
great grandmother	l'arrière-grand-mère
grandchildren	les petits-enfants
grandson	le petit-fils
granddaughter	la petite-fille
uncle	l'oncle
aunt	la tante
great uncle	le grand-oncle
great aunt	la grand-tante
nephew	le neveu
niece	la nièce
cousin (male)	le cousin
cousin (female)	la cousine
parents-in-law	les beaux-parents
father-in-law / step father	le beau-père
mother-in-law / step mother	la belle-mère
son-in-law / step son	le beau-fils
daughter-in-law / step daughter	la belle-fille
half brother / step brother	le demi-frère
half sister / step sister	la demi-sœur

Conversation deux

Gérard	D'où viens-tu ?	Where do you come from?
Sophie	Je viens des États-Unis. Et toi ?	I come from the United States. And you?
Gérard	Ma famille vient de la Côte d'Ivoire. Je m'appelle Gérard.	My family come from the Ivory Coast. My name's Gérard.
Sophie	Je m'appelle Sophie. Qu'est-ce que tu étudies ?	My name's Sophie. What do you study?
Gérard	J'étudie l'histoire parce que je veux être professeur d'histoire au lycée.	I study history because I want to be a high school history teacher.
Sophie	J'étudie la musique. J'espère jouer un jour dans un orchestre.	I study music. I hope to play in an orchestra one day.
Gérard	Quel instrument ?	What instrument?
Sophie	Je joue du violon.	I play the violin.

Vous venez d'où ?

To talk about where we come from, we can use the verb **venir** (to come). Here are the different forms of the verb:

je	viens	I come **or** I am coming
tu	viens	you come **or** you are coming (informal)
elle / il	vient	she / he comes **or** she / he is coming
nous	venons	we come **or** we are coming
vous	venez	you come **or** you are coming (formal / plural)
elles / ils	viennent	they come **or** they are coming

To use **venir** in a sentence, we combine it with the preposition **de** (from):

Ma famille vient <u>de</u> la Côte d'Ivoire

(My family comes <u>from</u> the Ivory Coast)

Je viens des États-Unis.

(I come <u>from</u> the United States)

When we use **de** before **les**, the two words are merged together to form **des.** When **de** is used before **le**, the same happens, and the words are merged to form **du**. However, when we use **de** before **la**, both words remain unchanged.

Les Nationalités

les États-Unis	the United States	
le Canada	Canada	
la France	France	
l'Espagne (f)	Spain	
la Suisse	Switzerland	
l'Italie (f)	Italy	
les Pays-Bas (m, plural)	the Netherlands	
la Belgique	Belgium	
l'Allemagne (f)	Germany	
l'Angleterre (f)	England	
l'Écosse (f)	Scotland	
l'Irlande (f)	Ireland	
le Portugal	Portugal	
la Grèce	Greece	
le Danemark	Denmark	
la Norvège	Norway	
la Suède	Sweden	
la Finlande	Finland	
l'Autriche (f)	Austria	

Le thème treize

Au camping (At the campsite)

L'alphabet

A – ah	B – beh	C – seh	D – deh	E - uh	F – eff
G – jjeh	H – ash	I - ee	J – jjee	K - kah	L – el
M – em	N – en	O - oh	P - peh	Q - kuue	R – air
S – es	T – teh	U - uue	V - veh	W – dooble-veh	X – eeks
Y - eegrek	Z – zed				

Conversation une

Pierre	Bonjour, nous avons réservé un emplacement pour notre camping-car pour une semaine.	Hello. We've booked a space for our camper van for one week.
Employé	Oui Monsieur, votre nom s'il vous plaît ?	Yes, Sir. What is your name, please?
Pierre	Je m'appelle Martin, ça s'épelle, M-A-R-T-I-N.	My name is Martin. That's spelled M-A-R-T-I-N
Employé	Oui, vous avez réservé pour cinq personnes et vous avez un chien.	Yes, you have reserved for five people and you have a dog.
Pierre	Nous avons trois enfants et un petit chien. Quand j'ai réservé l'emplacement, j'ai demandé si nous pouvions être près du club enfants.	We have three children and a small dog. When I booked the pitch, I asked if we could be near the children's club.
Employé	En effet, vous avez le meilleur emplacement de tout le camping. Il est situé prés du club mais aussi près des installations sportives.	As a matter of fact, you have the best pitch on the whole campsite. It is near the club, but also near to the sports facilities.
Pierre	Fantastique, J'ai oublié un sac de couchage, vous en vendez ?	Fantastic! I've forgotten a sleeping bag, do you sell them?
Employé	Oui, nous vendons des sacs de couchage dans notre magasin. Vous avez besoin d'autre chose?	Yes, we sell sleeping bags in our shop. Do you need anything else?
Pierre	Nous avons également besoin de charbon pour le barbecue. La douche du camping-car ne fonctionne pas. Où est le bloc des douches s'il vous plaît ?	We also need some charcoal for the barbecue. The shower in our camper van doesn't work. Where is the shower block, please?
Employé	Vous trouverez du charbon dans le magasin. Et pour les douches, il y en a juste a coté de votre emplacement.	You'll find charcoal in the shop. And for the showers, there are some just next to your pitch.

Conversation deux

Pierre	J'ai lu sur la brochure que la rivière est à cent mètres du camping. J'aime bien pêcher, j'ai besoin d'un permis de pêche ?	I read in the leaflet that the river is a hundred metres away from the campsite. I like fishing, do I need a fishing licence?
Employé	Oui, nous vendons des permis à la semaine. Vous en voulez un maintenant ?	Yes, we sell licences during the week. Do you want one now?
Pierre	Oui, je vais en acheter un. Combien ça coûte s'il vous plaît ?	Yes, I'll buy one. How much does that cost, please?
Employé	Ça fait quinze euros s'il vous plaît. Aussi, il y a la plage à deux cent mètres du camping. Les enfants peuvent jouer au volley et aussi il y a des animations pour eux.	That'll be fifteen Euros please. Also, there is a beach two hundred metres away from the campsite. The children can play volleyball, and there is also entertainment for them.
Pierre	Ah oui, mon fils adore faire des châteaux de sable et mes filles adorent ramasser des coquillages.	Ah yes, my son adores making sandcastles, and my daughters love collecting seashells.
Employé	Si vous avez besoin de pelles et de seaux, j'en vends ici.	If you need buckets and spades, I sell them here.
Pierre	Non merci, j'ai tout ce qu'il faut pour eux jouer à la plage. Est-ce qu'il y a des sauveteurs à la plage s'il vous plaît ?	No thank you, I have everything we need to play on the beach. Are there any lifeguards on the beach?
Employé	Oui la plage est surveillée et il y a un centre médical s'ils se font mal. Quels sports pratiquez vous ?	Yes, the beach is supervised, and there is a medical centre in case anyone has an accident. What sports do you do?
Pierre	Moi, le seul sport que je pratique est la plongée avec tuba. Mes enfants voudraient essayer la plongée sous marine.	Me, the only sport that I do is snorkelling. My children would like to try scuba diving.

Les passe-temps et les intérêts

To talk about our hobbies and interests, we use the verbs **jouer** (to play) and **faire** (to do or to make). Here are the different forms of **jouer** in the present tense:

je	joue	I	play / am playing
tu	joues	you (informal)	play / are playing
il/elle/on	joue	he/she	plays / is playing
nous	jouons	We	play / are playing
vous	jouez	you (formal)	play / are playing
ils/elles	jouent	they (m/f)	play / are playing

To use **jouer**, we also need to use **prepositions**. These are just small, one-syllable words that can have a variety of different meanings in different circumstances. With **jouer**, we mostly use the preposition **à**:

Je joue aux échecs

(I play chess)

In the example above, **à** would be placed next to **les**, so that the sentence reads **je joue à les échecs**. However, whenever we need to use an **à** and a **les** next to each other, we use **aux** instead. This is called a **contraction**. Here is a complete list of the contractions we use with **à**:

à + le = au

à + la = à la (this form does not need to be contracted)

à + les = aux

Here are some more examples of how these forms of **à** are used in a sentence:

Tu joues au basket. (this uses à + le = au)

(I play basketball)

Elle joue aux jeux vidéos (this uses à + les = aux)

(She plays video games)

Sometimes we also use the preposition **de** with **jouer**. This can be contracted like this:

de + le = du

de + la = de la (this form does not need to be contracted)

de + les = des

de is used with **jouer** like this:

Il joue de la musique

(He plays music)

We also use **faire** (**to do** or **to make**) to describe our hobbies and interests:

je	fais	I	do / am doing
tu	fais	you (informal)	do / are doing
il/elle/on	fait	he/she	does / is doing
nous	faisons	We	do / are doing
vous	faites	you (formal)	do / are doing
ils/elles	font	they (m/f)	do / are doing

Sometimes we use **à** or **de** with **faire**, and sometimes we don't use a preposition at all. Here are some examples of the use of **faire** in sentences:

Nous faisons du vélo.

(We cycle.)

Vous faites la cuisine.

(You cook – formal version.)

Le vocabulaire

English Object or Activity (noun)	French Object or Activity (nom)	English Action (verb)	French Action (verbe)
board games	les jeux de plateau	to play board games	jouer aux jeux de plateau
card games	les jeux de cartes	to play card games	jouer aux jeux de cartes
draughts	le jeu de dames	to play draughts	jouer au jeu de dames
chess	les échecs	to play chess	jouer aux échecs
darts	les fléchettes	to play darts	jouer aux fléchettes
pool	le billard	to play pool	jouer au billard
video games	les jeux vidéos	to play video games	jouer aux jeux vidéos
word games	les jeux de lettres	to play word games	jouer aux jeux de lettres
basketball	le basket	to play basketball	jouer au basket
cycling	le vélo	to cycle	faire du vélo
hockey	le hockey	to play hockey	jouer au hockey
skiing	le ski	to ski	faire du ski
football	le foot	to play football	jouer au foot
swimming	la natation	to swim	faire de la natation
tennis	le tennis	to play tennis	jouer au tennis
cooking	la cuisine	to cook	faire la cuisine
crocheting	le crochet	to crochet	faire du crochet
crossword puzzles	les mots croisés	to do crosswords	faire des mots croisés
dancing	la danse	to dance	faire la danse

fishing	la pêche	to go fishing	aller à la pêche
gardening	le jardinage	to garden	faire du jardinage
hiking	la randonnée	to go hiking	faire de la randonnée
jigsaw puzzles	le puzzle	to do a jigsaw	faire un puzzle
jogging	le jogging	to go jogging	faire du jogging
music	la musique	to play music	jouer de la musique
reading	la lecture	to read	faire de la lecture
sailing	la voile	to sail	faire de la voile

Le thème quatorze

Le déménagement (Moving house)

Conversation Une

Agent	Bonjour, Monsieur, Madame, asseyez-vous, s'il vous plaît.	Hello Sir, Madam. Please take a seat.
Pierre	Merci. Bonjour.	Thank you. Hello.
Agent	Puis-je vous aider ?	How can I help you?
Pierre	Nous cherchons un appartement de cinq pièces.	We're looking for a five room (four bedroom) apartment.
Agent	À acheter ou à louer ?	To buy or to rent?
Pierre	Nous voulons l'acheter pour nous, nos trois enfants, et notre chien.	We want to buy one for us, our three children, and our dog.
Agent	Quelle zone préféreriez-vous, avez-vous une idée ?	What area would you prefer, have you got an idea?
Pierre	Nous voudrions qu'il soit près de la Grande Place, si vous en avez quelque chose.	We would like it to be near the Main Square, if you have something there.
Agent	Donc, vous recherchez une zone centrale.	Ok, you're looking in the centre of town.
Pierre	Oui, c'est ça.	Yes, that's right
Agent	Je comprends, je cherche maintenant quelque chose pour vous. Désirez-vous un appartement dans un immeuble récent ou ancien ?	I understand. I'm now searching for you. Do you want the apartment to be in an old or recently built building?
Pierre	Pas très ancien et pas nécessairement récent.	Not too old and not necessarily recent.
Agent	Voilà, j'ai trouvé un situé à cinq minutes de la Grande Place, dans un immeuble construit en deux mille.	Here we go! I've found one which is five minutes from the Main Square, in a building that was constructed in 2000.
Pierre	Euh, c'est assez récent. Comment est-il équipé ?	OK, that's quite recent. How is it laid out?
Agent	Il a une salle à manger et quatre chambres à coucher, une salle de bains, une cuisine, un balcon, un vestibule, c'est-à-dire une surface totale de cent dix mètres carrés. Il coûte cent mille euros négociable.	It has a dining room and four bedrooms, a bathroom, a kitchen, a balcony, and an entrance hall. In total, it has a surface area of one hundred and ten metres squared, and the asking price is a hundred thousand euros.
Pierre	Oui, parfaitement. Nous voudrions le visiter.	That's perfect! We'd like to visit it.

Les grands nombres

seventy	soixante-dix (septante in Belgium, Canada, and Switzerland)
eighty	quatre-vingt (huitante in Belgium, Canada, and Switzerland)
ninety	quatre-vingt-dix (nonante in Belgium, Canada, and Switzerland)
one hundred	cent
one thousand (1,000)	mille
one hundred thousand (100,000)	cent mille
one million (1,000,000)	un million
one billion (1,000,000,000)	un milliard
one trillion (1,000,000,000,000)	un billion

Conversation deux

Sandrine	Il est vraiment beau et spacieux et la zone est justement ce que nous cherchions depuis longtemps.	It's really beautiful and spacious. And the area is exactly what we've been searching for for a long time.
Agent	Et le prix est bon, à mon avis. Désirez-vous l'acquitter par l'intermédiaire de la banque ou en espèces ?	And the price is good, in my opinion. Would you like to pay in cash or with a mortgage?
Sandrine	En espèces, c'est parfait. Les enfants seront enchantés !	In cash. It's perfect! The children will be delighted.
Agent	Alors, je vous attends ce soir à dix-huit heures, pour signer le contrat de vente-achat avec le propriétaire.	So, I'll expect you this evening at six o'clock to sign the sale-purchase contract with the owner.
Sandrine	Parfaitement, merci beaucoup, Monsieur ! Vous êtes très gentille !	Perfect. Thank you, Sir! You are very kind!
Agent	De rien, on se revoit à dix-huit heures !	You're welcome. I'll see you at six o'clock.
Sandrine	À plus tard !	See you later!

Le passé composé

Le passé composé, or the present perfect, is one of the main tenses we use to describe the past in French. It is formed by using an **auxiliary verb** (**avoir** or **être**) with the **past participle** of the verb (action word) that describes what is happening. It is formed like this:

J'ai trouvé un situé à cinq minutes de la Grande Place.

(I have found one situated five minutes from the main square.)

In this example sentence, the **auxiliary verb** is **avoir**. As the subject of the sentence is **je** (**I**), that means we use **j'ai** for **I have**. The next word that follows, **trouvé**, is the past participle of the verb **trouver** (**to find**). Here are some more past participles of verbs that you may have encountered, which use **avoir** as their auxiliary verb:

Infinitive of French Verb	Infinitive of English Verb	Past Participle	Passé Composé with 'je'	English Meaning of Passé Composé
habiter	to live (in a place)	Habité	j'ai habité	I lived / I have lived
payer	to pay	Payé	j'ai payé	I paid / I have paid
aider	to help	Aide	j'ai aidé	I helped / I have helped
laisser	to leave (an object somewhere)	Laisse	j'ai laissé	I left / I have left
manger	to eat	mange	j'ai mangé	I ate / I have eaten
suivre	to follow	Suivi	j'ai suivi	I followed / I have followed
voir	to see	Vu	j'ai vu	I saw / I have seen
vouloir	to want	voulu	j'ai voulu	I wanted / I have wanted

Some verbs use **être** as their auxiliary verb:

Infinitive of French Verb	Infinitive of English Verb	Past Participle	Passé Composé with 'je'	English Meaning of Passé Composé
partir	to leave (a place)	parti	je suis parti	I left / I have left
aller	to go	allé	je suis allé	I went / I have gone
venir	to come	venu	je suis venu	I came / I have come

Le thème quinze
Le temps (The weather)

Conversation Une

Sandrine	Ah, quel temps ! Il pleut des cordes depuis le matin.	Oh, such weather! It has been raining cats and dogs since the morning.
Pierre	Ah, tu es toute mouillée ! Va vite te changer sinon tu vas attraper froid ! Je vais te préparer du thé.	Oh, you're all wet! Go and change quickly, otherwise you'll catch cold! I'll make you some tea.
Sandrine	Oui, tu as raison, je me change et je reviens.	Yes, you're right. I'll change, and I'll come back.
	Un peu plus tard…	*A little while later…*
Pierre	Voilà, ton thé au gingembre. J'ai aussi préparé des éclairs au chocolat, tu en veux ?	Here you go, you're ginger tea. I've also made some chocolate eclairs. Do you want some?
Sandrine	Ah, merci ! Oui, volontiers !	Oh, thank you! Yes, gladly!

Le vocabulaire

Il fait beau	The weather is nice
Il fait mauvais	The weather is bad
Il fait chaud	It is hot
Il fait froid	It is cold
Il fait du soleil	It is sunny
Il fait orageux	It is stormy
Il y a des nuages	It is cloudy
Il y a du vent	It is windy
Le ciel est clair	The sky is clear
Il pleut	It is raining
Il neige	It is snowing

To ask what the weather is doing, you can say:

Quel temps fait-il ?

Conversation deux

Véronique	Maman, te voilà !	Mum, there you are!
Sandrine	Véronique, tu as l'air heureuse ! Qu'est-ce qu'il y a ?	Veronique, you look happy! What's the matter?
Véronique	Enfin, les examens sont terminés et ce sont les vacances ! Et tu m'as promis un voyage à Cannes.	Finally, the exams are over and it's the holidays! And you promised me a trip to Cannes!
Sandrine	Ah oui, je m'en souviens !	Oh yes, I remember that!
Véronique	Alors, on part quand ?	So, when do we leave?
Sandrine	Je vais voir avec l'agent de voyage et je te préviens.	I'll check with the travel agent and let you know.

Puis, sur la télévision…

Présentateur	Bonsoir à tous et à toutes et bienvenue au bulletin météo !	Good evening everyone, and welcome to the weather forecast!
	Au nord de la France, le temps est toujours nuageux, le ciel sera couvert !	In the north of France, the weather is still cloudy, the skies will be overcast!
	L'après-midi, il y a une alternance entre soleil et nuage !	In the afternoon, it will alternate between sunny and cloudy!
	Les températures varient entre dix degrés et douze degrés.	Temperatures will vary from ten to twelve degrees.
	Par contre, le week-end s'annonce mal pour le sud-ouest du pays.	On the other hand, the weekend looks bad for the south-west of the country.
	Deux départements sont en vigilance orange. Il s'agit d'un vent très violent avec des rafales de plus que cent kilomètres par heures.	Two départements are on orange alert because of very violent winds with gusts of over a hundred kilometres per hour.
	Donc, une tempête s'annonce sur Cannes et Toulon.	So, a storm is brewing over Cannes and Toulon.
	Veuillez ne sortir pas de vos domiciles ! Et restez bien à l'abri !	Please do not leave your homes! And stay safe!

Conversation trois

Véronique	Ah non, quel dommage !	Oh no, what a shame!
Sandrine	Ne sois pas triste ! On ira à Cannes une autre fois.	Don't be sad! We'll go to Cannes another time.
Véronique	Mes vacances sont déjà gâchées !	My holidays are already ruined!
Sandrine	Mais qui a dit ça ? On peut changer de destination. Que dirais-tu d'un séjour aux Alpes, en Suisse ?	But who said that? We can change the destination. What would you say about a trip to the Alps, in Switzerland?
Véronique	Oui, absolument !	Yes, absolutely!

Le thème seize

L'utilisation du pronom 'on' (The use of the pronoun 'on')

Nous et on

So far, during your French learning experience, you have used the word **nous** to mean **we**. However, there is another word that can mean **we**; the pronoun **on**. On is a more **informal** way of saying **we**, and it is being used more and more often in modern spoken French. If you are with friends, you would always use **on** instead of **nous**. **Nous** is reserved for more formal situations; when you would be using **vous** and not **tu**.

But how do we use **on**? The most important thing to remember is that we use it like **il** and **elle**, that is to say, **on** uses the same verb forms as **il** and **elle**. For example:

Il est français et il est aussi américain.

(He is French and he is also American.)

On est français et on est aussi américains.

(We are French and we are also American.)

The only difference between the two sentences above, besides the use of **on**, is that we had to add an **s** to the end of **américains** to make it plural. **Français** does not require an **s** to make it plural as it ends in an **s** already. Notice how the equivalent word for **is** and **are** is the same in both sentences; it is **est**. Here is a complete verb table for **être** (**to be**), including **on**:

Je	suis	I	am
Tu	es	you (informal)	are
il/elle/**on**	est	he/she/we	is
Nous	sommes	we	are
Vous	êtes	you (formal)	are
ils/elles	sont	they (m) / they (f)	are

If you look up a verb in the dictionary, you might see the **il/elle** form listed as **il/elle/on**.

Here are some example sentences which use **on** instead of **nous** to mean **we**.

1. Olivier et moi, on est mariés.

    Olivier and I, we're married.

2. On habite en Bretagne, en France.

    We live in Brittany, in France.

3. On est à côté de la mer, c'est chouette !

    We are close to the sea, it's great!

4. On fait du tennis, du jogging et de la natation…

    We practice tennis, jogging and swimming…

5. On a une fille qui s'appelle Leyla.

    We have a daughter named Leyla.

6. On écrit des livres audio qui enseignent le français moderne.

    We write audiobooks which teach modern French.

7. On voit souvent notre famille.

    We often see our family.

8. On voyage souvent : on a de la chance !

    We travel often: we are lucky!

9. On a une vie simple et on est heureux.
    We have a simple life, and we are happy.

On fait son devoir…

Using **on** as an informal version of **we** is only one of many functions it performs in French. The second one we are going to look at is its use as an **indefinite pronoun**, that is, it is used the way a king or queen might say **one does one's duty** as a general way of talking about **people** doing their duty. In modern English, we don't tend to use **one** for this purpose very much, instead we tend to use **we** or **you**. For example:

You've got to laugh, haven't you?

(People in general have got to laugh.)

Here are some example sentences:
1. On est poli ici.
   You are polite here.
2. On mange son diner avec une fourchette et un couteau.
   You eat your dinner with a knife and fork.
3. On ne sait pas jamais !
   You never know!

Le thème dix-sept
Les prépositions de lieu (Prepositions of place)

sur	on	
sous	under	
devant	in front of	
derrière	behind	
entre	between	
à côté de	beside / next to	
dans / dedans	in / inside	
autour	around	

dur – hard.

le sol – the floor.

Le thème dix-huit

L'impératif (The imperative)

Giving Instructions.

Garde-à-vous !

Levez-vous et écoutez !	Get up and listen!
Garde-à-vous !	Attention!
Ne bougez pas !	Don't move!
Déplacez !	Move!
Dépêchez !	Hurry!
Halte !	Halt!

L'impératif

When you want to give instructions in French, you need to use the **imperative**. There are three forms of the imperative; a formal form, an informal form, and a plural form. To use the formal and informal versions, we need to know the **vous** and **tu** forms of the verb you want to use to give an instruction:

Pronoun	Imperative Form of Travailler (a verb which ends in er)	English Meaning	Imperative Form of Partir (a verb which ends in ir)	English Meaning	Imperative Form of Perdre (a verb which ends in re)	English Meaning
vous	travaillez	work	partez	leave	perdez	lose
tu	travaille	work	pars	leave	perds	lose

Note that when using the **tu** form of a verb ending in **er**, you take the **s** off the end of the word. Here are some examples of how the imperative is used in a sentence:

Travaillez plus dur !

(Work harder!)

Pars ! Sinon tu vas être en retard !

(Leave! Otherwise you'll be late!)

Perds le match !

(Lose the match!)

In addition to the formal and informal versions of the imperative, there is also a plural form. This is the equivalent of saying **let's** in English. To use this form, we need the **nous** version of the verb:

Pronoun	Imperative Form of Travailler (a verb which ends in <u>er</u>)	English Meaning	Imperative Form of Partir (a verb which ends in <u>ir</u>)	English Meaning	Imperative Form of Perdre (a verb which ends in <u>re</u>)	English Meaning
nous	travaillons	let's work	partons	let's leave	perdons	let's lose

Here are some examples of this form of the imperative being used:

Travaillons plus dur !

(Let's work harder!)

Partons ! Sinon on va être en retard !

(Let's leave! Otherwise we'll be late!)

Perdons le match !

(Let's lose the match!)

As ever with French, there are some **irregular** forms of the imperative. These are:

Pronoun	avoir	être	savoir	vouloir
vous	ayez	soyez	sachez	veuillez
tu	aie	sois	sache	veuille
nous	ayons	soyons	sachons	veuillons

Here are some examples of these being used in a sentence:

Sois sage.

(Be good.)

Veuillez fermer la porte.

(Please shut the door.)

Sandrine, ayez confiance en vous !

(Sandrine, have confidence in yourself!)

Le thème dix-neuf
Les journées et les mois (Days and months)

Les journées de la semaine

lundi	Monday
mardi	Tuesday
mercredi	Wednesday
jeudi	Thursday
vendredi	Friday
samedi	Saturday
dimanche	Sunday

To say **on Monday** or **on Saturday** etc, we use **le**. For example:

Le lundi, je vais aller au cinéma.

(On Monday, I'm going to go to the cinema.)

Les mois de l'année

janvier	January
février	February
mars	March
avril	April
mai	May
juin	June
juillet	July
août	August
septembre	September
octobre	October
novembre	November
décembre	December

To say **in January** or **in June** etc, we use **en**. For example:

En juin, je vais aller en France.

(In June, I'm going to France.)

Des autres phrases utiles

la semaine (noun)	the week
le week-end (noun)	the weekend
le mois (noun)	the month
hier (noun)	yesterday
demain (noun)	tomorrow
prochain (m) / prochaine (f) (adjective)	next
dernier (m) / dernière (f) (adjective)	last

Take care when using **prochain/prochaine** and **dernier/dernière**; as these are adjectives, they must match the noun they are describing in terms of their gender. For example:

La semaine prochaine.

(Next week – *semaine* is feminine)

Le mois prochain.

(Next month – *mois* is masculine)

La date

To talk about the date, we can use the following construction:

Le + day + number + month

For example:

Le vendredi vingt-quatre février.

(Friday 24th February.)

Note that we say the French equivalent of **twenty-four** February rather than **the twenty-fourth of** February. To ask on what date someone has their birthday, we can use the following question:

Quelle est la date de ton anniversaire ? (for use in informal situations)

or

Quelle est la date de votre anniversaire ? (for use in formal situations)

Activité

In **le thème dix**, we looked at **le futur proche** (**the near future**) and how to use it. Using this tense, tell your partner one sentence about each of the following:

1. What you are going to do at the weekend.
2. What you are going to do next Tuesday.
3. What you are going to do tomorrow.
4. What you are going to do in December.
5. What you are going to do next month.

In **le thème quatorze**, we looked at **le passé composé** (the present perfect) and how to use it. Using this tense, tell your partner one sentence about each of the following:

1. What you did last weekend.
2. What you did last Thursday.
3. What you did yesterday.
4. What you did in March.

5. What you did last month.

Index of Vocabulary Topics

Small numbers	4
Ordinal numbers	7
Furniture	9
Food	13-14
Packaging and quantities	16
Adjectives to describe food	17
Clothes	20
Colours	21
Drinks	23
Animals	28-29
Adjectives to describe animals	30
In a doctor's appointment	32-33
Parts of the body	34
Directions	38
Possessive adjectives	41
Stationary	42
Family	44
Nationalities	46
The alphabet	47
Hobbies and interests	51-52
Large numbers	54
Past participles	55
Weather	56
Prepositions of place	61
Days of the week	64
Months	64
Other times and durations	64

Printed in Great Britain
by Amazon